Published by:
Dudley Publishing House (DP House)
An imprint of The Dudley Agency
www.dudleypublishinghouse.net

ISBN: 9798987671573

This book is a work of nonfiction based on the author's personal experiences. Some names and identifying details have been changed to protect the privacy of individuals.

Cover design by: DP House Creative Team
Interior design and formatting by: Dudley Publishing House

Printed in the United States of America
First Edition: 2026

For permissions, inquiries, or bulk orders, contact:
cindy@minimalistcindy.com

Table of Contents

Acknowledgements

This is the hard part. I can't list every single person who has supported me or inspired me to live a unique lifestyle. I know I will leave somebody out, and then there will be hurt feelings. I would like to thank all my friends, even those who aren't a big part of my life anymore. All of you have shaped me and molded me in so many ways. Your support means more than you'll ever know.

I'd also like to throw a shout out to the naysayers and the doubters. Trust me, they're out there. There's something rewarding about proving people wrong. There is satisfaction in not following the crowd and standing alone, at times.

I'd love to thank my close friend Melanie, who actually prompted me to write on the topic of being a homeless nomad. She has found the whole experience interesting and often asks me questions about it. She has taken a strong interest in those who are neurodivergent, and I'm able to provide her with first-hand knowledge, which helps her excel in her career in the medical field.

There are a few other close friends who do deserve special recognition. I'd like to thank Nancy Kuehn, Lindsey Morris and Lori Sturgill for taking a special interest in my life.

Nancy gave me the idea and the resources in finding pet sitting gigs. Both of us take a special interest in experiencing the entire world, meeting new people and loving animals. Neither one of us has a desire to live up to society's idea of a perfect life, and we aren't afraid to stand out and do our own thing.

When I found out I was neurodivergent, Lindsey was the first friend who was willing to have an in depth conversation about it. You were allowed to ask all kinds of questions and took a special interest in trying to understand. You never brushed me off or made me feel less than, even though you don't understand everything. That support means more than you'll know.

Lori, her husband Chris and I have dreamed about seeing the world together. We have fully supported each other through life's struggles. When I broke the news to Lori I was AuDHD, her reply was "That makes sense. So much is adding up." It's been a non-issue, and I was treated with so much understanding. You're a badass, and I love it.

I would like to thank the staff at Hope Community Church, along with care night leaders Phil and Christine LaFon, for making me feel at home in a new area. I've grown so much from the messages delivered at Hope and don't feel out of place worshipping there.

I'd like to thank Linda Thompson for choosing me to care for Cooper. Your wise decision helped bring me to the Carolinas, a home I love. Thank you to Linda's neighbor and best friend Marja Houston for helping out with Cooper and for guiding me while I got accustomed to life in the Carolinas.

I can't forget Angie and Tom Miller and Mildred Blackwell in Ohio. You folks opened up your home to me and let me be part of your family. Not many people would be willing to do that. You allowed me to live out my dream. I firmly believe that it was God led and you will be blessed for it.

My cousin Mitch Monson has been a best friend and like a brother to me. You always take the time to listen to my ideas. You're not afraid to ask hard questions to make me think, and you will offer your honest opinion when asked, even if it's not what I want to hear. You're not afraid to dish out positive feedback, which I appreciate. There's nobody's opinion I trust more than yours.

I'd also like to thank my sixth-grade teacher, Lorraine Martinson, posthumously. You were my favorite, and you were the one who planted the seed that I should start writing. You followed me all through my newspaper career and sent me letters of encouragement.

My sports editor, Lou Babiarz, at the Bismarck Tribune did a lot of the polishing and turned me into a much better writer. Lou was the best boss I've ever had at any job, and I miss the years when I was part of his staff. If I could rewind to an era, I would pick my years at the Tribune. You have inspired me more than you'll know. I'm so blessed that we have continued to carry on a friendship. You also share my love for heavy metal bands. Rock on, dude.

The staff at Dudley Publishing House rocks. Thank you for being willing to publish this book and working with me through the whole process. Book writing and newspaper writing are two separate skills.

Foreword

There are people you meet in life who simply get it—get you. Cindy is one of those people for me. From the beginning of our friendship, she made an impression. She was present, attentive initially quiet as she engaged in the act of listening. Wearing her head bandana, tattoos and all, her presence was known. She never demanded your attention but her intentions to know you, understand, and if lucky enough, to be your friend, were clearly present. Her mind and ability to express thoughts into written words has always been admired from the very beginning. Cindy is the type of friend with an easy rhythm. We can pick up where we left off with no judgement or pressure. Maybe it's our shared love of travel, animals (especially dogs), Motley Crüe and other 80's rock bands, or our mutual desire for growth and authenticity. Whatever it is, there's always been something both grounding and expansive about being in Cindy's orbit.

When she first told me that she was giving up nearly everything—her home, her furniture, all of her physical anchors—and hitting the road as a nomadic minimalist, my response may have been different than most. I didn't think it was crazy. I thought she was brave. In fact, I thought, "of course she is, this totally fits." Because underneath Cindy's direct, quirky, no-nonsense approach to life is a woman with remarkable intentionality. Every part of her journey— physical, emotional, spiritual and geographical —is rooted in purpose, even when that purpose wasn't yet clear. She wasn't running away. She was running toward something. That's what made sense to me.

I've done a bit of that myself—picking up and traveling far outside my comfort zone, seeking a new chapter in my own life. Something that doesn't have a name until you live it. And like me, Cindy learned that traveling solo doesn't mean that you're alone. It means you're giving the space to the voice inside that we often ignore as we are busy in our daily lives. Watching her chase that voice, that clarity and ultimately that freedom—I could not help but cheer her on. I loved following her whereabouts like a personal game of Where's Waldo. One minute she was house-sitting cats in Ohio, next she is in the sweltering heat of Florida checking out baseball games, and even off to Poland traveling and of course, intentionally connecting with people wherever she goes. Cindy's journalism background certainly stands out in knowing how to ask questions, engaging people to discuss their lives from their own perspectives and sharing their experiences. Add in some of her quirky sayings, perhaps from her North Dakota upbringing, and that is Cindy. Honest. Surprising. Intentional with her relationships, full of faith and daring to challenge herself to move towards her inner voice guiding her along the way.

This memoir you are about to read is a reflection of that same honesty and intentionality.

Cindy does not sugarcoat. She writes like she speaks—direct, witty, and deeply reflective, and always entertaining. What makes her voice so powerful isn't just the way she can turn a phrase (which she can), but her vulnerability and authenticity that shines through. She allows herself to be fully seen—fully, courageously, in all stages of becoming. She is relatable in so many ways. This book isn't about her losing over 100 pounds. It is about her shedding limiting beliefs. Shedding who she thought she had to be so she could finally become who she actually is.

And that self is still evolving. That's the beautiful part about Cindy and about life.

Along the way, Cindy has come to understand herself in ways that many people never allow

themselves to. She writes about her AuDHD—
Autism and ADHD. As someone who has lived
decades of often feeling misunderstood, she
does not shy away from learning about herself,
she seeks it out. Too often people with
neurodivergence are often shoved in to boxes
that don't fit. This can lead to "feeling too
much" or "not enough" at the same time.
Cindy's insights will challenge you, move you
and hopefully see the richness in stories that
defy stereotypes.

She talks a lot about community in this book—
how she needed it, how she built it, and how
she found belonging on the road and within
herself. I think that's why this book matters so
much right now. We are all, in some way trying
to find our people. Our space. Our peace.

Cindy reminds us that it doesn't always come in
the form we expect. Sometimes, it looks like
selling all your belongings. Sometimes, it looks
like sitting quietly with cats in a quiet house in
Ohio. And sometimes, it looks like taking that
step forward on faith as it maps out your next
step.

If you've ever wanted permission to leave the
life that no longer fits you... if you ever felt like
you were meant for something more, but didn't
quite know how to begin... or longing for

someone to say "I see you and I get it," — then this book is for you.

Let it take you where you didn't know you needed to go.

— Kathy Lawrence

Introduction

Living Light, Living Free

There's a certain freedom in hitting the road with nothing but a suitcase, a backpack, and a direction. No trailer hitched to the back, no "stuff" weighing me down—just me, a lead foot, and a sense that God was steering the wheel more than I was. That freedom didn't happen overnight. It was a journey of letting go—of possessions, of plans, of people's opinions—and it led me straight into a life I never expected but always needed.

I didn't write this book because I think my story is particularly extraordinary. I wrote it because, somewhere between chasing simplicity and chasing God, I found something worth sharing. I found a life that feels light and good and whole—even without all the usual things we think we need to feel that way. No mansion, no five-year plan, no Pinterest-perfect setup. Just peace. And peace, my friend, is priceless.

Before you turn the page expecting a how-to guide on minimalism, let me warn you—I'm not here to tell you to throw out your blender or live in a van down by the river (unless you want to). This isn't a manual. It's a memoir. It's about shedding the weight of expectation and learning to live freely, joyfully, and a little unconventionally. It's about faith, about following God's nudge—even when it doesn't make sense—and trusting that He's got a better plan than anything we could map out.

You'll find a bit of everything in these pages: a woman with AuDHD—autism with ADHD— learning to navigate the world on her own terms, a health coach figuring out what healthy *really* means, and a traveler who traded square footage for soul expansion. There are awkward moments, beautiful ones, hard ones, and holy ones. And through it all, God's fingerprints are everywhere.

I didn't always know this kind of life was possible. I used to chase stability like it was the finish line, trying to check off all the boxes of what "success" looked like. But the truth is, the more boxes I checked, the heavier life felt. It wasn't until I unclenched my grip on control, comfort, and comparison that I discovered something far better: clarity, purpose, and space to breathe.

What I've learned is this—joy doesn't live in cluttered closets or packed calendars. It lives in stillness. In surrender. In late-night prayers and road trip drives. It lives in doing things solo when others wait for permission. It lives in trusting that if God called you to it, He'll walk you through it—even when you can't see the next step.

Now, don't get me wrong—this isn't one big sermon. I'm just a practical, Jesus-loving, thrift-store-shopping gal who got tired of pretending I was happy with a life that felt too small. So, I made a change. A big one. And this is the story of what happened next.

This book is for the wanderers, the weary, the seekers, and the skeptics. It's for anyone who's ever wondered if there's more to life than keeping up and holding on. Spoiler alert: there is. And you don't have to have it all figured out before you take that first step.

So, if you've ever felt called to something simpler, something braver, something holier— welcome. This is a story about freedom. Not the kind you buy on vacation or glimpse in a weekend retreat. The kind you build when you start living for real, living for God, and living like you've got nothing left to prove.

Let's begin.

"Looking back, the signs were there... God was tapping me on the shoulder."

Chapter 1

The Tug Before the Leap

Looking back, the signs were there long before I packed up my SUV and handed over my condo keys. God was tapping me on the shoulder for years—but I kept brushing Him off with a polite, "Maybe later." You see, I'm the kind of person who likes order. A plan. A spreadsheet, if we're being honest. So, when He started nudging me out of my structured North Dakota life, I didn't exactly leap—I clung. White-knuckled.

I wasn't unhappy. That's what made the whole thing more complicated. I had a good rhythm going. I was coaching from home, working at Seeds of Hope Thrift Store part-time, and attending a church I liked. I even had a gym I actually used. Sure, I was single, over 40, and still figuring out what was next, but overall, life felt safe. Manageable. But deep inside, there was a quiet discontent I couldn't shake. Like I was wearing clothes that didn't quite fit anymore.

That internal itch only grew louder. I'd find myself walking through my condo and thinking, *Why do I own all this stuff?* Or I'd glance at the calendar and wonder, *Is this really how I want to spend my days?* The sense of misalignment wasn't dramatic—it was subtle, like trying to sleep on a mattress with one spring poking you all night. You can survive it, but eventually, something's gotta give.

I started talking to God more about it. Not just in my morning devotionals, but in the middle of laundry, while driving to the store, in random moments at the thrift shop. "Lord, am I missing something? Is there more You want from me?" I'd ask. And almost every time, I'd feel that same tug in my spirit. Not a voice, exactly, but a deep knowing: *Yes. There's more. But you'll have to leave this behind to find it.*

That terrified me. Leave *what* behind? My condo? My job? My routine? The Cash Wise Foods that was five minutes away and always fully stocked with my favorite dill pickle sunflower seeds? I had created a comfortable little life in Bismarck. It wasn't flashy, but it was mine. Letting go of it felt reckless. Irresponsible. Downright un-American.

But the tug persisted. It showed up in unexpected places—like in a podcast I stumbled on about nomadic living, or a conversation with a friend who had house-sat in New Mexico and couldn't stop talking about the freedom she felt. I'd smile and nod while secretly wondering, *Could I do that? Could I really just… go?*

Then, slowly, confirmation started to stack up. Coaching clients would say things like, "You have such a flexible lifestyle—you could live anywhere." Friends would ask, "Have you ever thought about traveling more?" One day, I walked into Seeds of Hope and had this overwhelming feeling that my time there was almost up—not because I didn't love it, but because God was calling me to release even the good things to step into the *right* things.

Still, I hesitated. It wasn't just fear—it was grief. The thought of leaving my routine, my gym, my church, my favorite gas station coffee (don't judge—it's better than most chains)… it felt like breaking up with a life I'd spent decades building. I kept asking God for one more sign, one more reason to believe this wasn't just a midlife crisis in minimalist clothing.

And then came the condo sale—the nudge that became a shove. I hadn't even listed it when someone offered to buy it, no haggling, just a showing, and then… done. It was too smooth to be coincidence. That's when I stopped fighting the current. I told God, "Okay, I'm in. Wherever You want me, I'll go." And for the first time in months, maybe years, I felt peace. Not the "everything is perfect" kind—but the kind that says, "You're exactly where you need to be—even if it doesn't look like it yet."

Leaving Bismarck didn't happen overnight. It was the result of a hundred small obediences stacked together, most of them terrifying. But each one made the next one easier. And eventually, the tug I'd felt for so long turned into a pull. A clear, undeniable invitation: *Come with Me. I have something better.*

And so, I said yes—not because I was fearless, but because I was finally done pretending that comfort was the same thing as calling.

Chapter 2

Journey of Faith and AuDHD

My journey with faith didn't start with fireworks—it started with a forced routine. My dad was a no-nonsense kind of guy who made it very clear: "We go to church." And when he said "we," he meant *all* of us. No excuses. No escape. As a child, I sat stiffly on the hard pews of a small rural Lutheran church, surrounded by hymnals and stained glass, trying to stay awake through sermons that felt like they'd been written by someone who'd never met a child with AuDHD. I didn't have a diagnosis back then—but believe me, the signs were all there.

We had to sit still. If we didn't pay attention, dad would thump us on the head with his big strong fingers. When we got older and sat with our friends, we had to pay attention or we were in trouble. The church was maybe 35 or 40 members and maybe 20 people showed up on Sundays. Our piano player was older than Methuselah and played off key. We had the typical church members: The ladies who took charge on Sundays who had lunch or coffee and told everybody what to do; the ladies who weren't in charge and complained about the other ladies; the people who sang off key; the people who overpowered everybody with their singing; the people who were out the night before but showed up hung over; the stiffs who frowned if somebody wasn't dressed properly; the dude who sneaked out to have a cigarette; the people who were always a sentence or two behind everybody else when reciting something.

Sitting still for an hour in those old wooden pews was like being in a straightjacket made of boredom. My brain would bounce from counting the ceiling tiles to wondering what was for lunch, all while the pastor's voice hummed on like a lullaby. Church was just something we *did*. I didn't understand it, but I obeyed. My autistic side craved the structure. My ADHD side hated every second.

Still, something about it planted a seed. It took root slowly, quietly. I didn't know then that faith isn't always born in big, dramatic moments. Sometimes it starts in the ordinary— week after week, sitting beside your family, singing hymns, watching your dad bow his head. My belief didn't fully come alive until years later, when God started showing up in unexpected places.

The shift began in my early 30s, when I became friends with Andrea, one of the basketball players that I covered as a sportswriter, and her entire family. Her name was pronounced "On-Dray-A." Her dad is Latino. I became friends with the whole family and carry a friendship with all of them to this day. That family welcomed me into their home and into their lives, and there was something different about them. They talked about God like they *knew* Him—not just as a distant figure from a pulpit, but as someone they spoke to, relied on, trusted with everything. They were born-again Christians, and they didn't just attend church—they *lived* their faith. That was new for me. Intriguing. And oddly comforting.

Through the Ronderos family, I started to see faith as more than a Sunday obligation. It was personal. Real. And deeply relational. Eventually, I stepped away from my Lutheran upbringing and began attending a Bible-based, non-denominational church. There was no memorized liturgy or forced tradition—just real people talking about a real God who offers grace, forgiveness, and love without conditions. That changed everything.

Faith became mine—not my family's, not my church's—*mine*. My relationship with Jesus became the anchor in a world that often felt chaotic and overwhelming. And trust me, my mind knows a thing or two about chaos. It wasn't until later in life that I learned the reason I always felt like I was walking uphill with roller skates: I'm AuDHD. A delightful little mix of autism and ADHD.

Getting that diagnosis in adulthood was like someone finally handed me the instruction manual to my brain. Suddenly, all the quirks made sense. My need for structure? That's the autism. My racing thoughts and tendency to forget where I set down my coffee five minutes ago? Pure ADHD. It was a relief, honestly. I wasn't broken—I was wired differently. Beautifully, uniquely, frustratingly differently.

The thing is, the world isn't always built for brains like mine. And faith? Well, faith requires stillness, trust, and surrender—all things that don't come naturally when your mind is running a mental marathon before breakfast. But God, in His kindness, meets me exactly where I am. In the noise. In the spinning thoughts. In the moments when I can't sit still or process emotions like everyone else. He's there. Always.

I've learned that having a neurodivergent brain isn't a curse—it's a gift, even when it doesn't feel like one. It means I feel things deeply. I notice what others overlook. I care hard. I love hard. I *live* hard. But I also need time alone, quiet spaces, and routines that help me feel safe. And that's okay. My faith gives me permission to be exactly who I am—a woman fully known and fully loved by a God who isn't overwhelmed by my overwhelm.

That foundation—faith and understanding my neurodivergence—shaped the life I live today. A life rooted in purpose, guided by grace, and stripped of the excess that used to weigh me down. It's the reason I'm able to live freely, travel boldly, and coach others toward wellness. Not in spite of my unique wiring, but because of it.

And as wild as my life has become, with all its twists and turns, I know one thing for sure: God's got me. He always has. From the dusty pews of that little country church to the winding roads I travel now, He's never let go.

Chapter 3

Labels, Late Diagnoses, and Liberation

When I was first told I had AuDHD, I wasn't surprised. I was *relieved*. Suddenly, so many moments from my childhood, my college years, and even my jobs made sense. It wasn't that I lacked discipline or drive—it was that my brain was wired differently. And not in a broken way. In a beautifully complex, occasionally chaotic way.

The ADHD and the autism findings came at the same time. So I discovered I had them both at the same time. I never lacked discipline or drive. In fact it's the opposite. So many people tell me they would love just a little bit of my discipline or drive. If my mind is set on doing something, I'll do it. For example, when I left college I put on a ton of weight. I made up my mind to lose it and dropped 107 pounds, and that led me to become a health coach. I thought it was simple to lose the weight. One of the adjustments I had to make as a health coach is not everybody will follow what they need to do to get healthy. For me, it was a simple straight path. I've always been driven to hit the gym, even when I was obese, I still worked out 5 or 6 days a week. Even in the N.D. winter when it was -40, I still went to the gym. If my mind is made up, I'm doing it.

In my 30s, I got out of debt. It was basically two years of not doing anything at all and finding free activities around town. I walked or rode my bike to the newspaper on days I didn't need to travel to an interview. I spent $10 in gas every three months because I only drove when necessary. I was disciplined to live extremely poor to get rid of my debt. Laser focused. That was my autism side coming out.

I struggle with people who say they want something and don't do anything about it. I struggle with people who say they're going to do certain things and then don't follow through. I take things literally. If I say it, I'll do it. I'm finding others say things just to say them and very few follow through. I've had to do a lot of personal development because I see a lot of people as "silly dreamers" or liars because they don't follow through. I've learned to take things that people say with a grain of salt. It's irritating, but I know how to wash my hands of it.

For most of my life, I followed the rules like they were gospel. I created structure, stuck to routines, kept things neat and tidy. Not because I was a control freak (though, sure, I had my moments), but because that structure kept me from feeling like the world was spinning off its axis. People thought I was disciplined. What they didn't realize was that those systems were survival.

Looking back, I see how often I forced myself to fit molds that were never designed for me. I beat myself up for not being more adaptable, more social, less intense. I wondered why certain things—like loud parties, multitasking, or surprise changes—left me exhausted or overstimulated when others seemed to thrive on them. Now, I know why.

I used to feel broken. Now, I feel *brilliantly designed*. Not because life got easier—but because I started understanding the wiring underneath it all. That knowledge gave me language for what I had always felt but couldn't explain. It gave me grace. It gave me freedom. And it gave me a mission.

Because here's the thing—God doesn't make mistakes. He didn't accidentally give me a neurodivergent brain and then forget to include the owner's manual. No, He made me intentionally. He gave me this specific mind for a reason. And now that I understand it better, I can work *with* it instead of against it.

As a health coach, that shift changed everything. I stopped trying to be the high-energy motivator type. That's not me. I'm the straight-talking, metaphor-loving coach who meets people where they are and helps them create a life that actually works for *them.* Neurodivergent or not. I coach from experience, not theory. From lived-in faith, not polished perfection.

I still struggle with certain things. Sensory overload in crowded restaurants. Actually, the sensory overload is a lot more than just crowded places. Noise from vehicles drives me insane. Any vehicle. The vehicles with loud mufflers and motorcycles are unbearable. It's actually physically painful. The sound of a whistle at any sporting event or the blaring of a horn is physically painful. Somebody playing videos on their phone sends me over the edge. The sound of a hand dryer in a restroom is physically painful for me to hear. People who are just loud in everything they do or loud talkers and laughers annoy me. I will still be nice to them but it's tough to take. With autistic people, it will likely make them irritated, angry, or will make them cry. Me? I get irritated. When

I reach sensory overload, then I'm angry. I've learned better how to manage this. I wear ear loops, which cancel out noise. It's not a cure all, but it helps. I'll also try to remove myself from the noise, if possible. Some people might think I'm being rude or that something is wrong, but it's necessary for me to do that. But now, I have tools. I have grace. And I have God—reminding me daily that I am not "too much" or "not enough." I am *His.*

Getting diagnosed later in life didn't change who I was—it just gave me permission to stop apologizing for it. I started advocating more openly, creating quieter spaces for myself, and saying no to things that drained me. And guess what? The world didn't fall apart. It actually started to make more sense.

So no, I don't see those labels as limitations. I see them as *liberation.* They're not cages— they're keys. Keys that helped me unlock deeper self-awareness, more authentic relationships, and a coaching style rooted in empathy and honesty. That's not just my diagnosis. That's my *design.*

Chapter 4

AuDHD Insights from a Health Coach

If I had a dollar for every time someone told me I "seemed so organized," I could probably retire early and buy a cabin in the Smoky Mountains. The truth is, I *am* organized—but not because I'm naturally wired that way. It's because I *have* to be. My brain, a lovely hybrid of ADHD and autism (AuDHD), functions like a computer with 37 tabs open at once—while streaming a rock concert and trying to make a grocery list.

I used to think I was just quirky. Or maybe high-strung. But later in life, when I finally received my diagnosis, it was like everything clicked into place. Suddenly, I understood why I'd rather follow a strict routine than wing it. Why loud restaurants or crowded rooms made me want to sprint for the exit. Why, despite being social and outgoing, I'd hit a wall and need total solitude to reset. It wasn't that I was being difficult—I was just managing a brain that processed the world differently.

When people hear "ADHD," they often picture a kid bouncing off the walls or someone constantly losing their car keys. And sure, I've lost a key or two in my day. But ADHD isn't just about being scatterbrained—it's about living in a constant tug-of-war between what your brain wants to do and what the world expects of you. Mix in autism, and that tug-of-war gets upgraded to an all-out battle. I thrive on structure, routine, and clear expectations. I follow rules like it's my full-time job. Change? Not my favorite.

Sensory overload is a real thing. Noisy environments feel like someone's turned the volume up on *everything*—voices, music, lights, even the texture of my clothing. I can feel overstimulated just walking into a busy Target. That's why the minimalist lifestyle became more than a choice for me—it became a lifeline. Less clutter means less chaos. Fewer distractions. More room to breathe. And let me tell you, breathing space is sacred.

Before I found my footing as a health coach, I spent over 20 years as a sports writer. Yep—AuDHD and journalism, an odd couple if ever there was one. But it worked. I thrived in the adrenaline rush of deadlines, the rhythm of games, the clear structure of stats and scores. Covering high school and college sports in North Dakota, I built a reputation. People knew me by name—some even knew me by byline. But being "on" all the time took a toll. Especially when people would corner me in grocery stores to gripe about the newspaper. I'd shop at midnight just to avoid the crowds—and the complaints.

Even as a reporter, I had routines to ground me. I wrote from the same spots, used the same kind of notebook, and had post-deadline rituals that helped my brain wind down. But as much as I loved writing, I could feel the burnout creeping in. I didn't want to live my life tethered to a desk or a deadline. I wanted more flexibility, more autonomy—and a way to help others feel as free as I was learning to feel.

That's what led me to health coaching. In a world that felt increasingly chaotic, it gave me purpose and peace. Helping others find health and wholeness became my new mission, and the beauty was—I could do it from anywhere. Beach, mountain, backseat of my SUV parked in a Planet Fitness lot. You name it. As long as I had Wi-Fi and a quiet corner, I was set.

Being a coach with AuDHD has made me more compassionate. Although I don't really get distracted from my goals. In some ways I can get distracted. I'll set out to do some errands, like get gas, pick something up at the store, and go to the post office. I might forget to do one of those tasks or I might leave the mail at home. I will tell myself I need to make a phone call after I finish a task, and I'll forget to make the phone call.

Minimalism helped too. It wasn't about getting rid of everything for the sake of it. It was about making space—for quiet, for purpose, for God. When I cleaned out my life, I could finally see what actually mattered. And what mattered wasn't the stuff in my house—it was the peace in my heart. I stopped keeping up with trends and started keeping up with grace. I let go of the noise so I could hear God more clearly.

So yes, my brain is different. And no, it's not always easy. But it's mine. And with God's help, I've learned to see it as a gift—one that lets me connect, create, and coach with heart. It's what led me to this life. A life that may look a little unconventional but fits me like a glove. A life that says you can be wired differently and still be whole. That you can have AuDHD and still live with intention. That you can be you—and still be free.

Chapter 5

Structure Meets Spontaneity

If there were a dating app for lifestyles, "structure" and I would've been in a long-term relationship. Early mornings, color-coded calendars, neatly stacked Tupperware—I loved it all. Structure gave me security. It helped my neurodivergent brain breathe. Without it, I felt like I was tap-dancing on a moving treadmill—blindfolded.

So, imagine the divine comedy of God calling me into a nomadic life—a lifestyle that, by definition, thrives on unpredictability. It was like asking a spreadsheet to go skinny dipping. And yet, that's exactly what happened. I, the girl who thrived on routines and Post-it Notes, traded it all for a life where "where are you sleeping tonight?" was a daily question.

I had peace about it. I didn't highlight routes or preload maps with spotty service. I didn't have that backup battery. I went in unafraid. God gave me that sense of peace that it would be OK. I just relied on GPS. I've never been afraid of getting lost or anything like that. You'll always come out somewhere, and snags will always work themselves out. I've always been able to utilize common sense, and that's all one needs when they head out!

But slowly, something beautiful happened. The structure didn't vanish—it evolved. I learned how to build rhythm into movement. Instead of knowing exactly what every day would look like, I created anchors: morning devotionals no matter where I was, coaching calls scheduled in time blocks, a dedicated "reset" day each week to regroup. My structure became portable.

That balance—of grounded habits within a flexible life—became my sweet spot. It's the only way I could function on the road without completely short-circuiting. I still needed my order, my systems, and my quiet corners. But now, they traveled with me, like a turtle with a Wi-Fi plan.

Spontaneity showed up too—uninvited at first, like a messy guest who forgot their toothbrush. But then it started bringing gifts, like a surprise visit to a tiny mountain church in Tennessee.

It was in those moments that I realized: structure and spontaneity don't have to compete. They can coexist. My structure helps me feel safe. My spontaneity helps me feel alive. And when they dance together—when I can pivot with peace because I've built in breathing room—that's when I feel most aligned with who God created me to be.

People often think living on the road is chaotic. And sure, it *can* be. There are missed exits, noisy parking lots, and the occasional wrong turn that leads you to a town with no coffee shop. (A true tragedy.) But for me, it's never been about chaos—it's been about trust. Trusting myself. Trusting my systems. And most of all, trusting God to meet me wherever I land.

If you had told me years ago that I'd one day find comfort in unpredictability, I would've laughed—loudly, awkwardly, and with a touch of panic. But here I am. A structured soul who now lives out of a suitcase, takes life one city at a time, and thanks God daily for the grace to live between the lines and outside them, all at once.

So yes, I still love a good planner. I still thrive on order. But now, I also thrive on faith, adventure, and the quiet confidence that even when the GPS fails and the Wi-Fi crashes, I'm still exactly where I need to be. And sometimes, structure looks like letting go just enough to be led.

Chapter 6

Nomadic Coach's Lifestyle Evolution

Most people have a "normal" timeline. Grow up, go to school, get a job, buy a house, settle down, and collect knick-knacks until the grandkids show up. But me? I've never really been a "normal timeline" kind of gal. The idea of settling down—like *really* planting roots—never felt quite right. Deep down, I always craved freedom. Movement. Adventure. But I didn't act on it until later in life. Until God nudged me—okay, shoved me—out of comfort and into the unknown.

It started with a whisper. That tugging from God that there was more to life than working five days a week, grocery shopping on Saturday night, and hitting the gym at the same time every evening. I had built a solid life in North Dakota—sports writer for over 20 years, part-time at a thrift store I loved, friends I adored, and a routine that felt safe. But safety can sometimes feel like a cage. And I was ready to break out.

The moment everything changed was subtle. My close friend Nancy had once told me about house-sitting gigs she took in New Mexico. I stored that nugget away, not realizing it would later become the spark that lit the fire. When I finally said yes to a three-month pet-sitting opportunity in Bolivar, Ohio, I told myself it was just a trial. "Three months," I said. "Just to see." But even before those months were over, I knew. I wasn't going back.

Ohio opened something in me. I felt free. I had structure—working remotely as a health coach—but I also had the flexibility to explore new places, try new coffee shops, meet new people, and see the world in a way I'd only dreamed of. The Millers, a kind-hearted couple I knew through coaching, let me stay in their home between gigs. That was God's provision right there—no question.

People often say, "I could never do what you do. I need security." And I get it. This lifestyle isn't for everyone. But for me, being tied down feels suffocating. I don't want a mortgage hanging over my head if it means giving up sunrises in the Carolinas, hockey games in North Carolina, or hiking trails in Tennessee. My security comes from knowing I can rely on God, my work ethic, and a backup plan or two. I don't float through life on faith alone—I also hustle.

I've always had multiple income streams. Even during my sports writing days, I picked up side gigs. When I became a certified health coach, I leaned into that with everything I had. My work goes wherever I go. I can coach someone from a beach, a mountain cabin, or the back of my SUV parked in a Planet Fitness lot. As long as there's Wi-Fi and a quiet space, I'm in business. It's not glamorous, but it's mine.

People sometimes assume I'm rich or that someone else is footing the bill for my travels. That makes me laugh. I live frugally. I shop at thrift stores, cook my own meals, and avoid buying anything I don't truly need. I don't care about brands or trends. I care about experiences—ones you can't buy at Target or wrap in a bow. Freedom is my luxury item.

Of course, not everyone gets it. Some people think I'm irresponsible. Some are envious. Others just shake their heads and mutter, "I could never do that." And you know what? That's okay. I didn't start this lifestyle to impress anyone. I did it because God asked me to let go—and I listened. I walked away from a condo, a community, and a predictable routine. In return, I got a life that fills me up in ways stuff never could.

Letting go of my belongings was one of the most freeing—and spiritual—experiences of my life. I donated, sold, or tossed nearly everything I owned. What didn't fit in my SUV got left behind. I kept a few sentimental tubs with my brother and cousin, but the rest? Gone. Because when you're not tied to "stuff," you're open to *everything*. Every day becomes a blank page. Every town, a new chapter.

I'm not saying everyone should quit their job and hit the road. But I *am* saying we all have something we're clinging to out of fear. For me, it was routine. Predictability. Familiarity. And the moment I released those things, I found joy, clarity, and more of God than I ever experienced sitting in my comfort zone.

This nomadic life? It's not a detour. It's the path I was meant to walk all along. Or in my case, drive.

"One of the first things you learn on the road is this: not all kindness is loud."

Chapter 7

Quiet Kindness, Loud Lessons

One of the first things you learn on the road is this: not all kindness is loud. Sometimes it's subtle. A stranger holding a door a few extra seconds. A barista adding an extra espresso shot "just because." A host leaving a hand-written note and your favorite snack waiting when you arrive. These moments might seem small—but they land big when you're living out of a suitcase and trusting GPS and prayer to get you where you're going.

What traveling taught me is something I actually learned much earlier in life—I just didn't know it at the time. When I was in elementary school, there was a boy in my class who… well, let's just say he didn't fit in. He was awkward, sometimes rude, always a little "off" by our small-town social standards. And, like most kids, I didn't understand him. I judged him. I was annoyed by him. Until one day, my uncle—bless him—pulled me aside and said, "Cindy, what if that boy is acting that way because life is really hard for him at home?"

That moment rewired something in me. It didn't excuse bad behavior, but it explained it. It softened my edges. And that one lesson has followed me through every chapter of life—especially now, as I travel and interact with so many people from so many walks of life. Whether I'm passing through a town in the Carolinas or grabbing gas in Georgia, I carry that lens with me: *You never know what someone's carrying.*

Empathy isn't loud. It doesn't make headlines. But it shapes everything—how I coach, how I interact with clients, how I navigate awkward social moments as someone with AuDHD, and how I respond when someone cuts in line or speaks harshly. I've learned that the most powerful response isn't always a comeback—it's compassion.

And sometimes kindness surprises you in the middle of your own mess. Like when I was in Bloomington, Illinois, when a mother and daughter told the waitress that they wanted to buy my dinner. They gave the impression that they couldn't afford much. I went over to thank them. Even though I was kind of in a hurry, I stood there and chatted with them for about 20 minutes to a half hour. They were Christians and asked how they could pray for me. I did the same in return. When I left the restaurant, I figured it out. All they wanted was my time.

They wanted somebody else's company; and me giving them my time meant the world to them. They had mentioned that a lot of people were always in such a hurry and nobody had time for them. They were grateful that I gave them my time. God taught me a lesson here. Even though I didn't want to take the time, I did. When I was done visiting with them, I was glad I had done it. As Christians we need each other. Solid relationships aren't built through texting or on Messenger. Actual conversations and meetings are something our society is missing.

Or when I was dog sitting in Louisiana. I went to an alligator farm. I made my reservation online as the farm got all kinds of tourists who passed through. I showed up at the same time a good looking younger man showed up. Turns out our last names were both Peterson and the lady at the counter thought we were a married couple. We both looked super confused. The lady went in the back to get our tickets. The guy said, "Want to play along?" I said, "Sure!" For the tour, we pretended we were newlyweds. I totally hit the jackpot on that one! Our tour director recognized us as newlyweds and the group clapped for us. One of the women in the group asked how we met. We totally played off each other. He started telling a made up story, and I added my bits and pieces in. It was chemistry. After the tour, when we left, he shook my hand and said, "This was fun," and then we shared a good laugh and went our separate ways. The funny thing is, I had no idea where he was from or where he was traveling. I knew zero about him. But for about an hour, we had a blast.

The truth is, the road can be lonely. Even when it's beautiful and freeing and full of adventure, there are moments when you wonder if anyone really sees you. That's when kindness matters most. It reminds you that God is always planting people in your path—people who reflect His love in tiny, tangible ways.

It's also made me more intentional about *being* that person for others. Whether I'm at the gym, at a gas station, or walking through a grocery store in a town I may never visit again, I try to carry empathy with me like a second skin. A compliment, a joke, a genuine "How are you?"—these things don't cost anything, but they can make someone feel like a million bucks.

I think about that little boy from my childhood often. I wonder where he is now. I hope someone showed him kindness. I hope someone gave him the benefit of the doubt.

Because that one comment from my uncle? It changed the trajectory of how I treat people. And now, I'm trying to pass that gift on, one quiet act at a time.

In a world that's always shouting, quiet kindness still speaks. And I'm convinced it's the language God uses most.

Chapter 8

Empathy From a Childhood Lesson

Empathy isn't something you learn in a textbook or from a self-help podcast. For me, it came when I was in Idaho, delivered by my uncle in a moment I didn't see coming—and never forgot.

I was just a kid, probably still figuring out long division and what exactly I was supposed to do with a curling iron. I'd come home from school frustrated about a classmate who, in my very mature adolescent opinion, was weird. He was just socially and physically awkward, smelled a little funky, smelled a little funky, picked his nose and ate it. He didn't get in trouble a lot. Just the opposite. He didn't socialize much because nobody accepted him.

My uncle wasn't the type to lecture, but something in my tone must've struck a chord, because he stopped me mid-rant. He said gently, "Did you ever think maybe he acts that way because of what he's going through at home? You don't know what kind of life he has behind closed doors."

I didn't respond right away. His words hit hard. In a single sentence, he introduced me to a truth I'd carry with me for the rest of my life: people are more than their behavior. What you see on the outside is often a shield—or a symptom—of what's happening on the inside. That boy's behavior wasn't about being difficult. It was about survival.

That conversation cracked something open in me. From then on, I started noticing people differently. I paid attention not just to what they did, but *why* they might be doing it. And that shift changed everything. I became more observant, more curious, and more compassionate—even as I continued to struggle with sensory overload and the chaos of navigating life with an undiagnosed neurodivergent brain.

It's probably no surprise that empathy became one of the cornerstones of my adult life and my work as a health coach. I don't judge people for their habits or their hang-ups. I know better. I've seen what unspoken pain looks like. I've lived it. And I know that sometimes, the loudest person in the room is the loneliest. Sometimes the snarky comments are really just masks for fear or trauma or exhaustion.

AuDHD didn't just teach me to be kind—it taught me to pause before assuming. And believe me, with ADHD and autism in the mix, I have to be *very* intentional about that pause. My brain likes quick conclusions and black-and-white thinking. But empathy asks us to sit in the gray and listen longer. To see the full picture, not just the snapshot.

Living a minimalist lifestyle has actually amplified this trait. When you're not bogged down by clutter—physically or emotionally—you have more space to truly *see* people. I've met folks from all walks of life on my travels. From baristas and pet owners to churchgoers and gym regulars. And each one carries a story you won't find on their Instagram profile. I've learned to ask questions. To be present. To make space for whatever someone needs to share.

My uncle probably doesn't even remember that conversation, but I do. It marked a turning point in how I relate to people. And it showed me that empathy isn't weakness—it's wisdom. The kind of wisdom that says, "You don't have to agree, but you can try to understand." And as a faith-filled woman trying to walk out her calling, I believe that's exactly what Jesus would do.

Looking back, I realize that empathy is what makes me a better coach, friend, and traveler. It's what helps me connect with people who feel misunderstood. It's what keeps me grounded when life gets noisy. And it's what reminds me, over and over again, that grace isn't just something we receive—it's something we offer, especially when it's hardest to give.

Chapter 9

The Space Between Safe and Strong

There's a strange ache that settles in your chest when you leave something safe—not because it was bad, but because it was familiar. That's what it felt like when I left home for college. It wasn't dramatic. No tear-filled airport goodbye, no shouting match with my parents. But there was a quiet grief under the surface. A knowing that things wouldn't be the same when I came back.

Growing up, I was incredibly close to my mom. We had our routines, our inside jokes, our shared love of predictability. She was my safe place. My soft landing. So when the time came to pack up for college in Minot, it felt like I was leaving behind not just a home, but a part of myself. I was excited, sure—but underneath the excitement was a slow-burn kind of fear. *Can I really do this on my own?*

My parents didn't beg me to stay, and they didn't encourage me to come back every weekend either. Looking back, I'm thankful for that. They let me go without guilt—which is probably the kindest thing they could have done. It gave me the space to find out who I was without the constant safety net. It was hard, but it was necessary.

That transition wasn't seamless. I had to figure out how to manage my time, cook my meals, and navigate social situations as someone with undiagnosed AuDHD. I didn't always get it right. I overcommitted. I burned out. I struggled to find a rhythm that worked. But through all of it, I kept showing up. Kept learning. Kept praying.

I realized pretty quickly that "strong" doesn't mean never struggling. It means knowing when to ask for help, when to rest, and when to keep going even when everything in you wants to curl up under a blanket and disappear. College didn't just teach me how to write or pass exams—it taught me how to live with myself. How to regulate my emotions, manage sensory overload, and advocate for what I needed, even when I didn't have all the right words yet.

I also learned that safety is a double-edged sword. It can protect you—but it can also hold you back if you're not careful. There's a point where staying "safe" starts to look a lot like staying stuck. And God, in His gentle but persistent way, kept nudging me toward something braver. Something deeper.

That nudge showed up in late-night journaling sessions, in walks around campus, in conversations with professors who believed in me. It showed up in my work as a sports writer, where I slowly began to understand my voice mattered—that I had something worth saying, even if I didn't always say it in the most typical way.

It wasn't glamorous. It wasn't fast. But I was building strength in that in-between space—the space between who I had been and who I was becoming. That space is where most growth happens. It's awkward and uncertain and full of growing pains, but it's also sacred.

Years later, when I packed up my SUV and drove away from North Dakota to live a more mobile life, it felt familiar. Not because it was easy, but because I'd already done the hard thing once: I'd left safe for strong. And that courage—that willingness to trust God with the next step—was born in a dorm room, not on a highway.

So if you're standing in that same space right now—between what's comfortable and what's calling you forward—know this: you don't have to be fearless to move. You just have to be willing. God will meet you in the in-between.

Chapter 10

College Transition and Independence

Leaving home for college is supposed to be this rite of passage—full of excitement, independence, and Instagram-worthy dorm decor. But for me, it felt more like ripping off a Band-Aid attached to my soul. I didn't just leave home that summer of 1989—I left behind a best friend. My mom.

We had a bond that ran deeper than the typical mother-daughter connection. We laughed and traveled together. She was my biggest cheerleader and, sometimes, the only one who really *got* me. So, when it came time to pack up and head to college, the emotions were heavy. I was ready for freedom, yes—but that didn't mean I wasn't heartbroken to go.

That transition was necessary. I knew that. My parents never guilt-tripped me into staying close. In fact, they encouraged independence, in their own North Dakota kind of way. They were old school—no hand-holding, no helicoptering. You figure it out, you pull your weight, and if you're unhappy, do something about it. That mentality was burned into me early on. Still, saying goodbye to my small-town life and my mom's gentle presence wasn't easy.

College was the first place where I started to really grow into my own skin. I made decisions on my own. Paid my own bills. Navigated dorm life, class schedules, and ramen dinners. I was learning what it meant to be an adult, which in college terms means staying up way too late, questioning all your life choices, and realizing your student loan money disappears faster than you thought possible.

One of the most important things I learned during that time wasn't in a lecture hall—it was the art of standing on my own. I missed my family, of course, but I also knew I couldn't cling to comfort if I wanted to build something of my own. My parents weren't the type to encourage me to come home every weekend. That just wasn't how they operated. Their style was: "Go, live, and figure it out. We'll be here when you need us, but we trust you can handle this." And in many ways, that trust became a silent push forward.

The more distance I had, the more I saw how their lessons had prepared me. I watched my parents hustle. They worked hard their whole lives, made do with what they had, and never depended on anyone else to solve their problems. My dad especially hated debt—and passed that down to me like a family heirloom. When I left for college, I knew one thing for sure: if I wanted something, I'd better earn it.

So, I did. I worked hard. I paid my student loans. I bought my own car—a real piece of work, but it ran. Most of the time. I wasn't handed anything, but I didn't expect to be. That mindset wasn't born out of hardship—it was born out of love. My parents loved me enough to let me struggle. They didn't make it easy. They made it *possible*.

Looking back, I can see how much that time shaped me. That painful stretch of letting go—of my mom, of familiarity, of the safety net—gave way to a deeper strength. I started trusting my instincts more. I started leaning on God more, too. When you're alone in a new city and your mom's not there to remind you where you put your laundry card, you learn to pray real quickly.

Even though we didn't talk every day, my mom was always with me. In the little sayings she'd repeat. In the way I organized my dorm room. In how I chose to show kindness to people around me. Our bond didn't disappear. It just shifted. Grew deeper, in a way that didn't rely on proximity.

The college years weren't easy, but they were mine. That stretch of life between "just a kid" and "full-blown adult" was clumsy, frustrating, and beautiful. And I wouldn't trade it. Not for all the clean laundry in the world. It's where I learned that I was capable. That I could make a life of my own. And that even from hundreds of miles away, a mother's love can still feel like home.

Chapter 11

Clocking In, Clocking Out

If someone had told me that clocking in at a newspaper sports desk, loading chips at Frito-Lay, and collecting debt would all prepare me for life as a health coach, I would've laughed—and not a cute, polite giggle either. More like a full-on, what-planet-are-you-on kind of laugh. And yet, every one of those jobs played a role in getting me here.

My career started with a bang—or more accurately, a box score. I was in college, working part-time as a sports clerk at the Minot Daily News. It was fast-paced, detail-oriented, and chaotic in the way that made sense to my brain. I didn't know it at the time, but those late nights fielding phone calls from coaches and writing up recaps were helping me build confidence, discipline, and a sharp eye for story.

I eventually became a full-time sports writer, and I genuinely loved it. Covering high school games, traveling for tournaments, interviewing athletes—it was demanding but satisfying. Still, the long hours, weekend work, and relatively low pay started to wear me down. I began to feel like I was living to meet deadlines instead of living to build a life.

So I pivoted. Or, if we're being real, I jumped ship and landed in a warehouse at Frito-Lay. I spent a year merchandising and navigating the kind of workplace politics that make you question the limits of your patience and hearing protection. It wasn't glamorous, but it paid better, and it gave me space to breathe— mentally and emotionally.

After Frito-Lay, I took a job in debt collections. Three years of listening to people cry, argue, or ignore you altogether will either harden your heart or soften it. Debt collecting actually kind of hardened my heart a little bit with all the stories people told that I knew were lies. It kind of made me lose my faith in humanity. Those who actually cared and didn't tell lies were the ones I felt empathy toward and made me willing to be flexible to help them.

I hated that job, to be honest. But I stayed because I needed the income and I was good at it. That's a tough combination to wrestle with— being effective at something that drains the life out of you. I used to pray, "Lord, please get me out of here," and every time, He whispered, *I will. But not yet.* So I waited. And while I waited, I learned.

Eventually, that "not yet" became a "now." Coaching started to grow. I began to realize I could help people not just meet their goals but understand themselves better. I could create a safe, encouraging space—something I'd longed for in so many of my own jobs. Coaching wasn't just a career shift. It was a spiritual realignment. I wasn't chasing titles anymore—I was following peace.

And here's what I've learned from clocking in and out of a dozen roles: every job teaches you something. Every frustrating boss, every mind-numbing task, every team meeting that could've been an email—it all adds up. It shapes you, equips you, and reveals what you *don't* want so you can finally recognize what you do.

Now, I coach from a place of understanding. I've been tired. I've been stuck. And because of that, I coach with compassion. I meet my clients where they are, because I've been there too—clocking in, clocking out, praying for something more.

So, no, this path wasn't linear. But I've come to believe that God doesn't do "linear." He does *layers.* And when you're faithful in the small things—when you keep showing up and doing the next right thing—He uses it all. Even the chip bags and cold call scripts. Especially those.

Chapter 12

Career Transition to Health Coaching

When people hear "health coach," they usually picture someone who lives off kale smoothies and runs five miles before sunrise. Spoiler alert: that's not me. I'm more of a coffee-before-cardio gal, and if I'm running, you'd better start running too—because something's probably chasing me. But becoming a health coach? That was one of the best decisions I ever made. Even if it took a few detours—and more than a few odd jobs—to get there.

My professional AuDHD journey started with a bang. Well, more like a byline. I was in college when I landed a part-time job as a sports clerk at a local newspaper. I wasn't entirely sure what I was getting into—I just knew I loved writing and I loved sports. That combo led me straight into a 20-plus-year career as a sportswriter. I worked for several newspapers in North Dakota and eventually became sports editor at the Minot Daily News. It was fast-paced, high-pressure, and, honestly, it suited me. My ADHD thrived on the deadlines. My passion thrived on the stories.

But here's the thing about working in newspapers: you don't do it for the money. Or the fame. Or the sleep. You do it because you love it. And I did—for a long time. I loved covering games, interviewing coaches, and capturing those moments of human grit and triumph. But the grind? It was relentless. The hours were long. The pay was laughable. And the stress of constant deadlines eventually wore me down.

By 2017, I knew I had to make a change. Walking away from journalism wasn't easy—it was part of my identity. But I also knew I couldn't keep sacrificing my health and peace of mind for a job that drained me. So, I left the world of sports writing, unsure of what was next but confident I couldn't stay where I was.

That confidence didn't exactly lead to a dream job right away. My first stop after newspapers was Frito-Lay, where I worked for about a year. Let's just say I learned quickly that merchandising chips wasn't my calling. After that came a stint in debt collections, which lasted three years. That job? Miserable. I had to call people who weren't honest, ask them for money that they knew they owed, and deal with stress that made my skin crawl. Every day I worked there, I felt like I was losing a little bit of myself.

But here's the thing about rock bottom—it often clears the way for something better. During that time, I began exploring health coaching. It was a field I'd been curious about for a while. I'd always cared about wellness—not just physical health, but emotional and spiritual well-being too. Becoming a certified health coach wasn't just a career move. It felt like stepping into a calling.

Suddenly, I was working from home, setting my own hours, and having real, meaningful conversations with people about their lives, goals, and health. The shift was incredible. My work became quieter, more intentional. I was no longer fielding angry calls about unpaid bills—I was helping people feel better in their own skin. And best of all, I could do it anywhere.

While building my coaching business, I also continued working part-time at a local thrift store, Seeds of Hope. That place was more than just a job—it was a grounding force. I loved the people. I loved the mission. I loved seeing people declutter and feel lighter, physically and emotionally. It fit perfectly with the minimalist lifestyle I'd embraced. The thrift store reminded me daily that most "stuff" doesn't matter—but people do.

My journey from sportswriter to health coach wasn't smooth or straightforward. It wasn't planned. But it was purposeful. God was redirecting me the whole time, even when I didn't see it. And in His grace, He used every single detour—every bag of chips, every debt collection call, every awkward step forward—to prepare me for the work I do now.

This career isn't about having it all figured out. It's about walking alongside people as they figure it out for themselves. And in doing that, I've figured out a few things too—like how freedom feels better than a paycheck, peace is more valuable than prestige, and serving people, heart to heart, is the most rewarding job I've ever had.

Chapter 13

Grace in the GPS Reroutes

When you live on the road, GPS becomes your co-pilot—right alongside Jesus. And let me tell you, between the two of them, I've had some *interesting* detours. GPS will get you where you *think* you need to go. Jesus? He'll take you where you didn't know you needed to be. And often, their routes don't match.

Grace.

That's what these reroutes have taught me: when your plan falls apart, God's grace shows up. Maybe not in the form of clear cell service, but in unexpected peace, unexpected kindness, and an even more unexpected sense that you are *exactly* where you're meant to be—even if your calendar didn't say so.

I have been rerouted lots of times though for various reasons. I can be frustrating, but it happens for a reason. Because of a reroute, I got to see the crash site of Lynyrd Skynyrd in Mississippi. A reroute led me in the direction of the World's Largest Paintball in Indiana, where I talked with the creator of it for about an hour. A retired gentleman who just loves to visit with people.

Traveling has a way of amplifying everything—your excitement, your anxiety, your sense of control, yet teach you all at the same time. Still, nothing tests your faith like being lost in a new city and a cranky GPS that insists you "turn left at the next opportunity" when there *is* no left. But it's also in those moments that I've felt the closest to God. When I can't rely on my own sense of direction, I lean harder into His.

It's not always dramatic. Sometimes grace shows up in a quiet parking lot where I can rest for the night. Other times, it's in the unexpected conversation with a stranger at a coffee shop who speaks something I needed to hear.

Not every reroute is physical. Some are internal. Emotional. Spiritual. Like the season when coaching slowed down and I started to doubt whether I'd heard God right in leaving Bismarck. Or when I found myself craving stability, wondering if I'd made a mistake living out of a suitcase. But every time I questioned, He confirmed. Not with booming voices, but with little moments. A smile from a client who made a breakthrough. A sunset over an unfamiliar skyline. Peace that didn't make sense.

The world says reroutes are delays. Detours. Wasted time. But God? He calls them refinement. Realignment. Redirection. Because often, we think we know where we're going. We have our destinations mapped and our dreams scheduled. But He's in the business of taking us deeper, not just further.

And what I've discovered is that the longer I travel, the more I trust the detours. Not because they're easy—but because they're sacred. They stretch me, humble me, and remind me that I'm not in charge (and that's a good thing). The reroutes are where the real growth happens—not on the straightaways.

So, now when my GPS says "recalculating," I smile. Because I know that somewhere up ahead, there's a lesson waiting. A grace I haven't seen yet. And a reminder that even when the route changes, the destination— God's purpose for me—hasn't.

Chapter 14

Travel Insights and Personal Growth

I've always believed the best education doesn't come from a textbook—it comes from a boarding pass. Give me a map, a tank of gas, or a plane ticket, and I'll show you more history, culture, and connection than any classroom can offer. That's not to downplay education. It's just that some things you have to *feel* to really understand. You have to walk the cobblestone streets, hear the different languages, taste the food, and meet the people. That's where the real learning happens.

I've been blessed to travel to 48 of the 50 states (I'm coming for you, Alaska and Colorado), and I've seen everything from the crash site of Lynyrd Skynyrd to the bright lights of Washington, D.C. I've pet sat in charming small towns, wandered through the Deep South, hiked in North Carolina, and found peace on Carolina beaches. Every city, every roadside stop, every minor league baseball game has taught me something. Mostly, that the world is way bigger than the bubble I used to live in— and way more beautiful too.

But one of the most powerful moments came far from home—in Gdańsk, Poland. I was visiting with a group and ended up on a boat ride, chatting with a local man who owned the boat. He wasn't flashy or loud, just a regular guy with weathered hands and kind eyes. As we floated along the Motława River, he told me about life under communism. About the scarcity, the fear, the constant surveillance. And then he smiled and said, "Freedom tastes different when you've lived without it."

That sentence hit me hard. It stayed with me long after I left Poland. We toss around the word "freedom" in the U.S. like it's just another buzzword. But for this man, freedom wasn't theoretical—it was tangible. Sacred. Earned. His words reminded me that the privileges I often take for granted—like traveling freely, choosing my job, expressing my faith—are monumental. Travel doesn't just broaden your horizons; it humbles your heart.

And while I love seeing landmarks and checking off bucket list items, the best part of travel is always the people. Whether it's the pastor at a tiny mountain church in Cosby, Tennessee, who still uses an overhead projector, or a barista in Forest City, North Carolina, who remembers your name and order, these moments stick.

These are the snapshots of real life that can't be staged or filtered.

Travel has also helped me embrace my personality more fully. I'm someone who prefers dry humor over small talk. I connect through storytelling, usually with a dash of sarcasm and a few offbeat analogies that sound weird until they land. I'm not big on clichés. Don't tell me to "just follow my bliss" or "live my truth." I'd rather say something like, "If you're paddling a canoe with a spoon, maybe it's time to reassess your equipment." It sticks better that way.

That style—quirky but real—isn't just how I speak; it's how I connect. When you've got AuDHD and a neurodivergent brain, clarity matters. So does authenticity. People want to be heard, not preached at. And whether I'm coaching someone through a lifestyle change or talking to a stranger at a baseball game, I've found that honesty, humor, and a solid metaphor go a long way.

The more I traveled, the more I realized I didn't need a massive house, a fancy wardrobe, or a high-powered title to feel fulfilled. I needed motion. Connection. Stories. I needed to be reminded that life is a patchwork of different cultures, backgrounds, and beliefs—and that God's fingerprints are on all of it.

And yes, I've made mistakes along the way. Like the time in New Orleans when I thought my SUV had been stolen, only to realize I parked it in a different lot. Or the time I spent the night in a Planet Fitness parking lot in Williamsburg, Virginia, and felt more refreshed the next morning than I did at most hotels. My lifestyle isn't fancy, but it's rich with experiences. And that's what I value most.

So if you ask me what I've learned from traveling, I'll say this: people are fascinating, freedom is sacred, humor is a bridge, and no amount of Pinterest-worthy decor can match the view from a mountaintop you climbed yourself. My travels aren't just about places— they're about becoming a fuller version of who God made me to be. One road trip, one conversation, and one spoon-paddled canoe at a time.

Chapter 15

Clutter, Clarity, and the Call to Release

Before I ever knew what minimalism was, I was already halfway there. I just called it "feeling smothered." I've never been one to chase designer handbags or clutter my shelves with collectibles, but somewhere along the way, stuff just... accumulated. And not just physical things—emotional weight, mental loops, unspoken expectations. My life looked tidy from the outside, but inside, I was carrying too much.

It wasn't until I was working at Seeds of Hope Thrift Store that I began to connect the dots. Day after day, I'd sort through donations, pricing items people once treasured and now wanted to be rid of. I'd listen to stories from shoppers—some looking to save money, others trying to fill a void. One afternoon, after processing five boxes of Christmas decorations from someone downsizing, I asked myself, *How much of what I own actually adds value to my life?*

That question haunted me in the best way. I started looking around my condo—at the books I never opened, the clothes I never wore, the knickknacks I dusted but didn't love. Why was I keeping all of this? Because I might need it someday? Because it was a gift? Because it represented a version of me I thought I had to hold onto?

The truth was, letting go of physical clutter was easy compared to letting go of the emotional kind. The "what ifs." The "shoulds." The idea that productivity equals worth. That a full closet meant I was prepared. That being surrounded by stuff made me safe. But God was inviting me into something simpler. Not just a clean house—but a quiet spirit.

It started with one drawer. Then a closet. Then the realization that if I was really going to live this mobile, faith-led life, I couldn't drag all this baggage with me. And not just in bins or boxes—but in beliefs. I had to let go of needing to be seen a certain way. I had to stop proving my value through possessions or packed schedules.

Minimalism, for me, isn't about bare walls and folding shirts into neat little squares. It's about alignment. About choosing what serves the life God is calling me to—and releasing what doesn't. That includes habits, relationships, and yes, even the three identical black tank tops I'd been hoarding "just in case."

As I let go of stuff, I gained clarity. It was like wiping a foggy mirror—I could finally see who I was becoming. I realized that freedom wasn't about being able to go anywhere. It was about not being weighed down by the things that kept me stuck. And peace didn't come from having a fully stocked pantry. It came from trusting God would provide what I needed, when I needed it.

Letting go wasn't always easy. Some things held sentimental value. Some carried guilt. But each item I released felt like a declaration: *I am not defined by this. I am free to move.* And that freedom created room—for joy, for calling, for unexpected adventures with God at the wheel.

So now, when people ask how I can live out of a vehicle or a suitcase, I smile. Because what I've learned is this: when your heart is uncluttered, you don't need much to feel full. The lighter my load, the deeper my faith. And I'd trade five storage tubs for one moment of true peace any day.

"I didn't just empty my condo.
I emptied myself."

Chapter 16

Trading Things for Freedom

People talk about minimalism like it's a trendy aesthetic—white walls, neutral bedding, and one lonely plant in the corner. But for me, minimalism wasn't about curating a "look." It was about creating a *life*—one where I could breathe, move, and focus on what really mattered. Letting go of things wasn't just a weekend project with donation bins and Pinterest boards. It was a soul-deep purge of everything I thought I needed to feel secure.

It started with one tub. I looked at it—full of college notebooks, outdated electronics, and random cords I couldn't identify—and I asked myself, "Why am I keeping this?" That one question turned into a flood. I started examining every drawer, every closet, and every dusty box in storage. And what I found was staggering. I had spent years collecting stuff I didn't use, didn't love, and honestly didn't even remember owning. So I let it go. Piece by piece. Bag by bag.

Now, don't get me wrong—I wasn't reckless Though I did toss family heirlooms—pretty much throwing away all the stuff I had from my mom—I did keep photographs, some WWII vouchers of my mom's and items like that.

I did get real honest with myself about what was serving me and what was just taking up space. In the end, I kept a few tubs with my cousin and brother—things that truly meant something to me—but the rest? Gone. Donated, sold, or trashed. And with every item I released, I felt a little lighter. A little freer.

Working at Seeds of Hope, a local thrift store, only reinforced what I already knew: most of us are drowning in stuff we don't need. I watched people donate entire carloads of items they once thought were important. Some were tearful. Some were relieved. Some were just making room for *more* stuff. But I always noticed the emotional weight behind every drop-off. Because we don't just collect things— we attach meaning to them. Sometimes healthy meaning. Sometimes not.

That store became more than a job for me. It was a quiet ministry. I wasn't just sorting donations or organizing shelves. I was witnessing people's stories—breakups, moves, cleanouts after a parent passed away. People didn't always say it out loud, but I could feel it. Letting go of things is never just about the things. It's about identity, memory, transition.

And sometimes, it's about finally saying, "I'm ready to move on."

Minimalism gave me room to move—not just physically, but spiritually. I didn't feel tethered anymore. I could pick up and go, knowing that everything I truly needed fit in my SUV. That kind of freedom is hard to explain to someone who's never lived it. It's not about owning less to feel superior. It's about owning less so you can *feel* at all. So you can hear God more clearly. So your mind and heart aren't constantly managing chaos.

Letting go was emotional at times. I'd come across old writing samples from my newspaper days, childhood mementos, gifts from people no longer in my life. And I'd feel a tug. A pause. But I'd ask myself: "Is this who I am now?" If the answer was no, I let it go with gratitude. Because it served me once—but it didn't need to follow me forever.

Some people don't understand why I chose this path. They assume I gave everything up out of necessity or crisis. But the truth is, I chose it. Deliberately. Joyfully. I chose a minimalist life because it gave me *maximum* peace. I didn't want to spend my time managing stuff. I wanted to spend it living, traveling, helping others, and hearing from God without all the background noise.

And let's be honest—there's something deeply satisfying about not having to move furniture or clean out a garage every six months. My needs are simple: coffee, Wi-Fi, and a place to sleep. Everything else is optional. That simplicity has become my sanctuary. A quiet rebellion against a world that says more is always better. I've found that better is found in *less.*

Minimalism isn't about deprivation. It's about direction. It's about choosing a life that aligns with your values, not your storage unit. For me, it's been a daily practice of asking, "What matters most today?" And more often than not, the answer isn't something I can buy. It's peace. Purpose. Freedom. And you can't put a price tag—or a receipt—on that.

Chapter 17

When the Nest Empties—So Do You

I didn't just empty my condo. I emptied myself.

That realization didn't come while boxing up the usual suspects—kitchen gadgets, picture frames, and that one drawer everyone has full of who-knows-what. It came the day I stood in the middle of my quiet, echoing living room with nothing left but a folding chair, my Bible, and a deep ache in my chest. That space had been full of my life for years—routine, security, memories. And now it was just... quiet. Strangely holy.

Letting go of my condo wasn't just about selling a place. It was about surrendering everything I thought defined me: my home base, my comfort zone, my last tether to what once was. I'd told God, "I'm ready for whatever's next." But as the space around me emptied, I realized He wasn't just clearing my schedule—He was clearing my soul.

There's something sacred about the in-between. When one chapter has closed, but the next hasn't begun. That space where your GPS says "recalculating," and you're not sure if you should turn left or just sit still. For me, it felt like standing in the doorway of a house I loved, knowing it would never be mine again—but also knowing that leaving it was an act of obedience.

People think minimalism is about decluttering. It is. But it's also about grieving. Because when you let go of things, you often let go of the identity they held. I wasn't just parting with furniture—I was parting with the version of Cindy who thought success meant stability. Who believed faith was easier in familiar places. Who equated safety with sameness?

And yet, in that emptiness, something unexpected arrived: peace. Not the "everything's figured out" kind. The *deep breath, holy hush, God's got this* kind. The kind of peace that only shows up when you've finally laid it all down. I didn't know where I was going next, but I knew I wasn't alone in the going.

Funny how the nest gets lighter right when you need to fly. When you've released all the things that gave you comfort—but also quietly caged you. That's when your spirit starts to soar—not in the absence of weight, but in the presence of trust.

It reminded me of the moment my parents let me leave for college. They didn't beg me to stay. They didn't hold on. They released me with love, even though I know it hurt. That's the kind of releasing God asks us to do too—with people, places, dreams. To hold them loosely. To love them fully. And then to let go when it's time.

I still carry that image of the empty condo with me—not as a loss, but as a landmark. A holy reminder of what happens when we make room. When we trade full shelves for full hearts. When we stop clinging and start trusting.

Because sometimes, God asks you to empty the nest—not so you can be left with nothing, but so He can fill you with something new. Something wild, unpredictable, and better than anything you could've built on your own.

Chapter 18

Faith, Signs, and Starting Over

I've learned that when God wants you to move, He usually doesn't whisper. He nudges. And then, if you're still ignoring Him, He'll start rearranging things so obviously that even your stubborn, overthinking, checklist-loving brain can't miss it. That's exactly what happened when He called me to leave North Dakota—the place I'd lived almost my entire life—and start over.

Let me be clear: I wasn't trying to run away. I wasn't unhappy. I had good friends, a church I liked, and a condo I owned. I had stability, routines. But I also had this growing sense that something was shifting. My spirit felt restless. My prayers became rawer: "God, if You want me to stay, I'll stay. But if You're calling me to something else, I need You to make it really, *really* clear."

Well, He did. In the fall of 2021, everything started pointing toward change. I had already left my old jobs—sports writing, then Frito-Lay, then the debt collections role that had drained me dry. Coaching had taken off, and I was working at the thrift store, but I started to sense that this season was winding down. I told a friend, "I feel like God is about to close a door. I just don't know which one." Within weeks, three different people—who knew nothing about each other—said something along the lines of, "You seem ready for something new."

Then came the condo. I'd been thinking about selling it for months but wasn't sure how or when. One day, I casually mentioned to someone that I *might* be thinking about selling. Two days later, they came back and said, "We want to buy it." No realtor, no listing, no sign in the yard. Just a handshake and an agreement that felt like it had been orchestrated in heaven. I took that as my green light from God. Actually, it was more like a flashing neon billboard: "It's time."

Even though I was scared, I had peace. That's how I knew it was God. I didn't feel frantic or uncertain. I felt ready. Sad, yes—but not hesitant. I knew I wasn't running *from* anything. I was walking *toward* something new. I packed my life into my SUV, said goodbye to my condo, and started driving. I didn't know exactly where I was going—I just knew God was already there, waiting.

Faith like that doesn't come overnight. It comes from years of watching God show up in little ways: a bill paid when money was tight, a job offer at just the right time, and a stranger with an encouraging word. It comes from wrestling with doubt, crying through disappointment, and still choosing to believe He's good. Every major move I've made in my life has been anchored in prayer. Not perfection. Not control. Just prayer.

When I left Bismarck, I had no concrete plan. Just a few pet-sitting gigs lined up and a sense that God would provide the rest. And He did. I found places to stay. I met people who felt like family. I discovered that freedom doesn't mean recklessness—it means trust. Every time I asked, "Lord, where next?"—He answered. Sometimes not until the last minute, but He always came through.

I often talk to God like He's sitting in the passenger seat next to me. (Which, let's be honest, with all my traveling, He pretty much is.) I'll say things like, "Okay, Lord, I need a quiet parking lot tonight" or "Can you help me find a clean bathroom and decent Wi-Fi?" And somehow, I always do. That kind of companionship changes you. It teaches you that faith isn't about performance—it's about presence. About leaning in and listening, even when the path doesn't make sense.

Starting over wasn't just about geography. It was about surrender. It was about finally letting go of the idea that success means settling down, collecting things, and climbing some invisible ladder. For me, success now means obedience. Peace. Knowing that I'm where God wants me—even if that place changes every few months.

I don't know where this road will ultimately lead. But I know Who's guiding it. And I'd rather follow Him into the unknown than stay stuck somewhere He's already left. That's not recklessness. That's faith. The kind that packs up everything, leaves the keys on the counter, and drives off with peace in your heart and Jesus riding shotgun.

Chapter 19

Finding Home Without a Zip Code

If you'd told me five years ago that I'd feel more at home in a borrowed house with a borrowed dog than in my own condo, I would've laughed and probably quoted my mailing address just to prove a point. But now? I'm learning that home has far less to do with where you park and far more to do with where you feel *held*.

That realization didn't hit me all at once. It came in moments—quiet, holy, ordinary moments. Like sipping coffee on a stranger's porch while watching the sunrise. Like curling up with Cooper, the dog I was pet-sitting in North Carolina, and realizing I hadn't felt that calm in weeks. Like walking into a local church as a visitor and leaving with hugs and lunch invites.

Turns out, you don't need four walls you own to feel like you belong somewhere. You just need peace. And when God is directing your path, that peace can find you anywhere—even in places you never thought to look.

I used to think home meant permanence. A place you anchored to. A mortgage. A mailbox. But now, I see it differently. Home is where your soul breathes easy. Where your spirit exhales. It's not about being settled—it's about being centered. And for me, that center has always been God. But I humbly have to say it's not "always" on God. Unfortunately, I make a lot of decisions and a lot of my actions don't always put God in the center. I need to grow in that area. I often let myself think that I know better or I don't slow down enough to listen to God. I'm definitely a work in progress and I make lots of mistakes in that area.

Everywhere I've been—from small-town North Dakota to the coastlines of South Carolina—I've carried the same quiet prayer: *Lord, is this it? Is this the place You're planting me?* Sometimes the answer was "not yet." Other times it was "just for now." And then there were those rare, sacred whispers of "Yes. Stay here a while."

That's how it felt in the Carolinas. It wasn't just the weather, or the landscape, or even the low cost of living. It was the people. The warmth. The way the community opened its arms without asking for a résumé. It was Cooper, of course—his goofy joy, his companionship, his silent reminder that presence matters more than possessions.

And it was the quiet voice of God saying, *You don't need a deed to be rooted. You just need me.*

Finding home without a zip code means being okay with movement—but also knowing when to pause. It means carrying your rhythms with you, but staying open to new ones. It means trusting that wherever you land, God has already gone ahead and prepared the ground.

I still don't know if I'll "settle down" permanently. I'm not sure I need to. What I know is that I've found a new definition of home—one that isn't bound by address changes or furniture sets. It's in the people God places in my path. In the stories He invites me to step into. And in the steady, anchoring peace of His presence.

So no, I don't have a zip code I claim. But I do have something better. I have direction. I have purpose. I have peace. And that, I've learned, is home enough for me.

Chapter 20

Cooper, Coffee, and Carolina Calling

Some people fall in love with cities. I fell in love with a dog—and then with a state. His name was Cooper, a dog with a soft face, soulful eyes, and a tail that could clear a coffee table in two swipes. I was pet sitting him in Boiling Springs, North Carolina, and I honestly thought it would be just another gig. Feed the dog, water the plants, keep the couch free of dog hair. I didn't expect to fall for the whole town.

Cooper was the kind of dog who made you feel like you were the most important person in the world just for walking through the door. We developed a routine: walks around the quiet neighborhood, 8:30 am coffee on the couch (for me, not him), and evenings curled up with a book or an episode of "say Impractical Jokers or Golden Girls." That dog didn't just keep me company—he anchored me. And I realized I didn't want to leave.

Boiling Springs was slower-paced than what I was used to, but in the best way. People waved when you drove by. And something about the air—the way it carried the sounds of cicadas among other things—made my soul feel at ease. I found myself lingering longer than usual. Extending my stay. Taking side trips to Forest City and other Carolina towns that felt like home before I even unpacked.

I met people who became instant friends—like they'd just been waiting for me to show up so we could get started. Some of them were coaching clients, others were fellow believers I met through local churches or gyms. We bonded over faith, coffee, and dry humor. (My love language.) These connections weren't surface-level. They were real. Rooted. The kind that felt like family without the shared DNA.

By then, I had lived out of my SUV for months. Traveled from Ohio to Florida or Washington, D.C. to Tennessee, picking up pet-sitting gigs, working from my laptop, and trusting God for each next step. I had loved the freedom. But in the Carolinas, something shifted. Freedom started to look like *belonging.* Like a place to come back to—not just pass through. For the first time in a long time, I felt like maybe I didn't have to keep moving.

I found a rhythm in Boiling Springs that surprised me. Morning coffee at home. Quiet walks with Cooper. Coaching calls from cozy corners of a borrowed house. I even had my own seat at a local church—nobody assigned it, but everyone knew it was mine. That kind of familiarity does something to your heart. It plants a seed.

Of course, I still had the itch to travel. That will probably never leave me. But now I knew I wanted a home base. A place to breathe between adventures. A town where I knew the grocery store layout and which parking lots were quiet enough to pray in. The Carolinas gave me that—without asking for anything in return.

Cooper wasn't mine to keep, but the peace I found while taking care of him? That stayed. His steady companionship during those weeks in Boiling Springs reminded me how healing simple things can be—routine, quiet, a good dog. And as silly as it sounds, I think God used Cooper to show me where I belonged. Sometimes divine direction comes in the form of wagging tails and muddy paw prints.

People ask if I'm "settling down" now, and I always smile. Not exactly. But I've planted roots—not the kind that hold you back, but the kind that give you strength to keep going. Roots in faith, in friendship, and in a part of the country I never expected to love so deeply. Shelby and the surrounding towns became more than a stop on my map. They became part of my story.

And it all started with Cooper. One dog. One ordinary gig. One unexpected homecoming. Now I live in Spartanburg, just over the border from Cooper and Boiling Springs. That's the beautiful thing about this journey—it keeps reminding me that joy often sneaks in when you're just trying to do the next right thing. You don't have to chase it. Sometimes, it comes running—with a leash in its mouth and a tail that won't quit wagging.

Chapter 21

A Letter to the Girl Who Was Waiting

Dear You,

You've spent a lot of years waiting—for permission, for clarity, for a sign. You've tried to do everything "right," followed the rules, played it safe, stayed in line. You've carried responsibility like a backpack filled with rocks—never complaining, just quietly adjusting the straps when they dug in too deep.

You've been faithful. You've been kind. And if I'm being honest, you've been *exhausted*.

I see you now, standing in your quiet condo, coffee in hand, and heart both full and aching. You want more—but you're not sure if that's selfish or holy. (Spoiler: it's probably both.) You feel the tug. You hear the whisper. But you're scared. You've worked so hard to build this life—what if tearing it down is a mistake?

Here's what I want you to know: letting go doesn't mean losing. It means *making room*.

You don't have to prove your worth by what you carry. You don't have to measure your faith by how little you ask for. You don't have to stay small so other people stay comfortable. God's calling you into something wider, wilder, and deeper—not because you're failing, but because you're ready.

I won't lie—it won't always be easy. There will be frustration and prayers that feel unanswered. You'll question the path. You'll miss the old rhythm. But then, somewhere in the middle of all that uncertainty, you'll feel it— peace. Not the kind you earn by checking boxes. The kind that shows up when you finally unclench your fists and trust Him.

And you'll laugh. Loudly. Often. In parking lots and coffee shops and churches you didn't plan to find. You'll meet people who remind you who you are. You'll write things that help others feel seen. You'll coach from compassion, not perfection. And you'll realize: this *is* the life you were always meant to live.

To the reader holding these pages: you're not too late, too much, or too far off course. Whatever tug brought you here—follow it. Don't wait for perfect timing or perfect faith. Just take the next brave step. And then the next. Let God fill in the rest.

You don't have to have a zip code to belong somewhere. You don't have to have a five-year plan to move forward. You just have to be willing. Open. And maybe a little stubborn in hope.

Keep walking. Keep trusting. Keep releasing what was to receive what's next.

I'll be cheering you on, always.

With love and light luggage,
Cindy

About the Author

Cindy Peterson was born and raised in Mylo, North Dakota. She graduated in four years from Minot State University, in North Dakota, with two bachelor's degrees in criminal justice and sociology. While attending college, she worked part-time in the sports department at the local daily newspaper. She soon realized she made a big mistake in the majors she chose, and she decided to stick with newspapers. Despite working for peanuts, she stayed in the industry for nearly 25 years, earning several awards for her writing. In 2005, she was named the North Dakota Associated Press Sportswriter of the Year by her peers.

Cindy left the newspapers and has been self employed ever since as a publishing power strategist for Dudley Publishing House and a health coach, Working from home has helped her manage her AuDHD, allowing her to be at her best each day while focusing on optimal health.

Cindy now lives in Spartanburg, South Carolina and enjoys hiking the mountains of South Carolina and North Carolina. Cindy loves traveling and exploring the whole world. She loves attending all sporting events, as long as a score is kept. She can be found at any college event in the Carolinas and is a season ticket holder for the Wofford men's basketball team. Cindy also patronizes the minor league baseball parks in the Carolinas. You will find heavy metal and yacht rock music from the 1970s and 1980s streaming from her car radio.

Cindy has a passion for helping all furry animals, especially her buddy Cooper. She attends Hope Community Church in Shelby, North Carolina, and loves spreading the word of God.